THE TRUTH ABOUT FAST FOOD

NUTRITION BOOKS FOR KIDS

Children's Diet & Nutrition Books

Speedy Publishing LLC
40 E. Main St. #1156
Newark, DE 19711
www.speedypublishing.com

Copyright © 2017

In this book, we're going to talk about why fast food isn't good for your health. So, let's get right to it!

F ast food, also called *junk food*, isn't good for adults or kids. It's convenient and saves time. It also saves cost. These are some of the reasons it's so popular. Fast food restaurants serve burgers, chicken, pizza, and tacos. Restaurants aren't the only source of *"fast foods."* If the *"food"* you're eating is a processed food from a package that you heat up quickly to eat, it probably falls into the *"fast food"* category as well.

"Fast Foods"

Most of the time these foods look appetizing and taste good, but things that taste good aren't always good for your body or your health! It's important for you to understand the truth about fast food.

Fast food is usually loaded with calories and sugar, but it has very few nutrients. If you eat junk food on a regular basis, it can be addictive. This is because a great deal of the food prepared has a lot of salt or sugar. Both of these types of ingredients increase food cravings, but aren't good for your health.

Eating junk food can make you obese. It can also make you chronically ill. It can even affect your mental health by lowering your self-esteem or by making you feel depressed. If you're not healthy, then you don't do well in school or in your extracurricular activities like sports.

People in the United States didn't always eat fast food. Before the 1950s, most meals were prepared at home. Not everyone ate the proper foods at home, but most people had a fairly balanced diet that wasn't loaded with fat, sugars, and too much salt. Today 25% of the people in the United States eat junk food on a regular basis. As a result, there is a huge increase in both obesity and the chronic illnesses it creates.

RISK FOR OBESITY

Many people in the United States, both adults and children, are obese. This simply means that they have too much body fat for their height. Eating fast food on a regular basis leads to obesity.

If you eat a healthy diet at home, you're getting a lot of vegetables, fruits, whole grains, and milk. These foods have lots of nutrition, fiber for your digestive system, and aren't too heavy in calories. However, fast food is just the opposite. It has very little nutritional value, which means it doesn't have many vitamins or minerals for good health. Instead, it's filled with too much fat, salt, and sugar.

Friends enjoying lunch.

It doesn't have much fiber, which is very important for good digestion. Even smaller portions of fast food have way too many calories and carbohydrates than healthier meals do. The fast food choices at restaurants that seem healthier, like salads, frequently have chemicals to preserve them and these are unhealthy as well.

Once you get into the bad habit of eating fast food, you tend to make poor choices when you eat at other meals too. The more high-calorie, processed foods you eat, the more addicted you become.

What Will You Pick? Healthy Food or Junk Food?

Eating the fast-food way becomes a habit and it's a habit that frequently leads to dangerous levels of obesity.

If you eat an extra 185 calories a day, every day, by the end of the year you'll be 6 pounds heavier.

CHRONIC ILLNESS

Obesity leads to many types of chronic illnesses. A chronic illness is one that lasts as long as three months or more. Some chronic illnesses can't be cured, but can only be treated, which means they last throughout your life. If you're obese as a child or teenager, you are more likely to have high cholesterol or heart disease when you get to adult age.

Scientific studies have shown that junk food increases your risk for deadly diseases, such as high blood pressure, stroke, or diabetes. The Center for Disease Control has predicted that if trends with fast food continue, by 2050 one in three people will have some form of diabetes, which can result in disability or death.

Studies at Harvard University have shown that obesity will reach an all-time high of 42% of all people in the United States within the next thirty years, if people don't change the way they eat. In other words, obesity is the result of eating too much fast food and having too much body fat can destroy your chances for living a healthy life.

SELF-ESTEEM AND DEPRESSION

When you're obese, it's difficult to have positive self-esteem and a sense of confidence. It's especially hard when other people tease you or bully you because of your body fat. If you're feeling down because of these factors, it can also lead to depression.

Studies from nutritional experts at the Mayo Clinic have shown that eating fast food can create feelings of depression even if you're not obese. The reason is that if you eat this way, you're not getting the proper nutrition.

Students in cafeteria line being served lunch.

Without the proper nutrition, you don't have the energy to do and enjoy the things you love. Good nutrition is critical, especially if you're still growing. If you're not getting the vitamins and minerals you need, it has a negative impact on your growth and development. Lack of nutrition can affect your ability to do well in school and in social situations too.

During your teenage years, you'll go through a lot of changes in your hormones as you go through puberty. This makes you vulnerable to mood swings. If you eat healthy foods, it helps you stay on an even keel and keeps your mental health stable. It's been shown that the trans fats and saturated fats in processed foods, whether you eat them at home or at a fast-food restaurant, increase the risk of depression by 58%.

Burger and French Fries.

Junk Foods.

ENERGY AND FOCUS

It takes a lot of energy and focus to do the things you need to do every day. You get up in the morning and get ready for school. Once you're at school, your day is really demanding as you learn new subjects and make new friends. When you come home, there are chores to do and homework to be finished. Then there are sports or other extracurricular activities that you enjoy and time with your family.

All of these actions take energy. Kids who don't get the right nutrition feel sluggish throughout the day. They become *"couch potatoes,"* which simply means they sit on the couch instead of doing fun physical activities. If you don't give your body the nutrition it needs, it won't perform at its best at school, during sports or other activities you love, and at home.

Obesity is a major cause of diabetes.

No Energy after eating Junk Food.

WHY DOES JUNK FOOD CAUSE DIABETES?

When you eat a lot of sugar that's been processed, the insulin levels in your body increase. Sugary drinks, like soft drinks and fruit juices with lots of added sugar, are unhealthy. Foods that are made with white flour that have almost no fiber aren't good as a steady diet. If you eat junk food throughout the day, you have such high levels of insulin that your body develops a resistance to insulin. Then, you are at risk to become obese or develop Type 2 diabetes.

Little Child eats fast food. Studies shows that over the past four decades, Fast foods especially among children and adolescents raised the risk of obesity.

Prior to the 1980s, it was unusual to see this type of diabetes in teenagers, but today 15% of the teenage population has this deadly disease. Poor diet with an increase in consumption of junk food has caused this alarming trend.

FAST FOODS ARE OFTEN HIGH IN SODIUM

One of the characteristics that many fast foods have is that they are very high in sodium, which is regular table salt. Salt is used as a food preservative, but when you cook fresh foods at home you eat a lot less salt than if you eat processed foods or a meal from a fast food restaurant. Too much intake of salt potentially causes hypertension, also known as high blood pressure. It can also contribute to diseases of the heart, kidney, and liver.

Salt and Potato Chips.

The everyday American eats five to ten times the amount of salt that is recommended by the United States Dietary Guidelines. Most people should have no more than 2,300 milligrams of salt daily and people who already have hypertension should only eat about 1,500 milligrams a day.

EAT HEALTHIER
FOR A LONG
LIFE
Stir fried vegetables.

Eating a burger with fries and a milkshake is okay once in a while. The problem is that many people eat this type of fast food diet every day or several types a week. A healthy diet has lots of vegetables, fruits, whole grains, and milk. The less processed foods you eat, the better.

Milkshake trio.

Even the so-called healthy choices at fast food restaurants, like salads of different types, frequently have harmful preservatives and chemicals. If you prepare your own food at home and follow the food group guidelines, you'll have a better chance at a healthier and happier life.

Awesome! Now you know more about why fast food is bad for you and why you should make healthy food choices. You can find more Diet & Nutrition books from Baby Professor by searching the website of your favorite book retailer.

Visit

BABY PROFESSOR
EDUCATION KIDS

www.BabyProfessorBooks.com
to download Free Baby Professor eBooks and view
our catalog of new and exciting Children's Books